THE INFINITE DIMENSIONS

IS THIS WORLD ILLUTIC? IS THIS WORLD REAL? IS THE M THEORY CORRECT?

HIMNISH BORA

Contents

The Basics of Dimensions

The Paradoxes

So, as we have learned about the simple and basic dimensions to the fourth dimension, let's start talking about the term paradoxes. Well the simple definition for paradox is that the time is changeable with the help of dimensions. Because the three basic dimensions- one dimensional, two dimensional and three dimensional are the basic dimensions for giving structure its shape. But, the other dimension's meaning is totally different. Because the other dimensions can mean to give you some abilities for every dimension. Like, for example, I am a structure made of four dimensional. Now that I will have some abilities like travelling in time. Now if I will go to the past and make any changes, then it will also affect the real time (present time) world. So if I will go to the past and give him something, then it will affect the history and the present time world and make changes to it. This concept is also known as the Paradox. Now let's talk about the basic beliefs of the people. Many people tend to part the dimensions to 11th (known as the M - theory). Let me first talk about the 5th dimension. Before our 5th dimension, the 4th dimension is also advanced from that of the 3rd dimension. But what is the difference between these two Dimensions 4th and 5th? The main reason is that the 4th dimension is only just imaginary. So, the fifth dimension has some energy and ability that helps you to travel to the past but doesn't give you to change any events as this is the base of all those other dimensions. It does only help you to view your past. But that small 4th dimensional space alone gives so much trouble to imagine what shape or thing it will take in it. So to imagine other dimensions is nearly impossible. Now, let's get to the 6th dimension. It is more advanced than the previous one. It will help you to not only travel back to time, but also make changes. But these changes will affect your present now. So, this says that the paradox also needs the help of dimensions to explain it. So now, let me explain the next dimension, the 7th dimension. This is obviously more advanced than the previous one. It will help to travel back time and make changes in it. But, the additional thing is that it will not affect the present. Now, let's head to the 8th dimension. It will not give you new abilities but give you a new unit for the shape. The 9th dimension will have the rights to view, change, and edit time. The 10th dimension, or the dimension where the gods live, have all the possible rights to manage everything. They can freeze, continue and take back time in any order. But the last, 11th dimension will be the creator of the universe who is the supreme power and has the rights to manage the universe and can destroy and create another universe and also, our universe can also be destroyed and created by the creator. These dimensions are shown in fig below. So, you have understood the concept paradox. So, changing the time will also affect the time in your present form. The paradox is under the hands of the ultimate dimension. This theory also explains that there is also another universe for the same universe. For now, we shall go to the next chapter, The Infinite Dimension.

CHAPTER THREE

The Infinite Dimensions

As we know about the dimensions very clearly, then we shall talk and discuss about the topic 'infinite dimensions'. As I have given some examples in the preface of this book, there is written that some supreme power had made us and we consider them as our god. But what if there is another energy, or creature that is even sumpremier than our considered god? That means that there must be another creature which is bigger than the god of the god. That means there may be more gods for one god. And because of this, we can know that the machines and robots (Artificial Intelligence {AI} Humanoid robots) are made by us. They also have a cpu chip card that acts as a brain for them. Then who made them? By us. So for the robots, we are the god for them. So, day by day, every generation is evolving something called dimensions because over the years, people have made various progresses and done so much for us. So, we are machines which are made by god. So the god that made us must also be made by other creatures. That means that every generation has its own dimension and it is growing day by day. Nevertheless, the creatures that made our god must be made by some mysterious creatures. And the mysterious creatures must also be made by some other creatures. But this only has one difference and that the other gods are more advanced than us and have very intelligent brains. They might also live in a different dimension than us. These dimensions must be growing from 3-10000 or even more (I mean infinite ∞). So, are there infinite dimensions? I don't clearly know but it has not even been solved by other scientists. But there is a very tricky question. Because every thing must have an ending but will it work for every possible array? Because is there a beginning where this infinite working started? If it is, who was and how can he be made? Who made that power that influenced everything to make infinite dimensions? There must be some very mysterious thing behind it. But if we are in 3rd dimension, then does this thing tell us that it is not much of a day to reach the end of dimensions or is it already ended with us or somewhere else? Finding these questions must be very hard because it is only hard to imagine a single four dimensional shape or space. It might be solved in the future but I can tell you that it might take 1000 years or even decades to solve it. But we now also have quite good evidence and knowledge about these infinite dimensions. But not enough to solve this mystery. But now let's talk about some theories that say that there are infinite dimensions. But wait, if there are infinite dimensions then there must be infinite universes. It also includes the theory of multiverse or many universes. But before that, let's talk about the theories that explain whether there are infinite dimensions or not. But the most trusted and well explained theory is only the theory of the multiverse. Is there many universes beyond our universe? Some of them say that there is no multiverse or many universes because present ideas can confront the one and only universe theory but do you think, like when we talk about seeing things with our telescopes and space telescopes, they are not that powerful to see what is beyond the universe. Are there many universes? Let's discuss in the next chapter.

CHAPTER FOUR

The 'Multiverse' Theory Or not?

Are many universes there or not? This theory is a little bit complicated. Many argue that there are many universes and there are some that say our universe is the only one here. It's kinda cool if we say that there is no multiverse nor the only universe. I am supposed to say Dualverse. My theory includes the theory of Dualverse. How can I say that the dual verse or Two-Universes exist? We know that every matter has its anti-matter. So, every particle has its antiparticle. Like every single thing created in this world has an anti and non anti or has antonyms. Like we can say our particle neutron - proton. As the neutron is the negative charge and proton is the positive charge. An additional example is Male - Female. So if there is a universe, there should also be an anti-universe. This proves the theory of Dualverse. For us, we see the other universe anti and if their life exists, then they will also see ours as anti. But there is a difference. Everything in this world has a difference. Like the antonyms good - bad also has a difference as the two words describe different meanings. Therefore negative matter or the negative universe is non visible or invisible matter and so the difference is they can see us but for us it's hard to detect. In CERN, there is the largest collider in the world where we can detect negative matter. Recently, a matter was detected called Ghost matter. I shall not talk about it right now so I am just saying that anti matter can be found with this collider. Let us just talk about the multiverse. Scientifically, the basic thought about these theories is that there exists a dualverse. But what about the multiverse? Basically, the multiverse is a mythical thought about it but there is a thing that the universe is infinite. But now a confusion arises. We are talking about infinite also, definite also, dual also, so what exactly is there. Dimensions have no anti or non-anti as they themselves form negative and positive matter. So this can be infinite. Matter has its anti matter so universe should also have its antimatter as the universe is also made of matter. Multiverse or dualverse? Well, talking with science, dualverse but talking with myth, multiverse. There should be an anti you, anti home, anti friends, anti gender, anti everything. It will be completely different or opposite of yours and your life. This science world also is made with the law of nature where nature has everything to control in this whole world. So, to enter a completely different world, you will have to take the permission of nature. Everything will be perfectly different so the other universe there doesn't have any laws of nature and you can break there. Even the impossible things here is possible in that universe. Like traveling in speed of light or cross its speed here is impossible, but in that universe, it is possible. They don't have any rules and can even do things that are fictional like they can change the map of the world. But as we have learnt this, there still question arises, is there infinite universes or two universes? So, mysterious! We can only do this if a theory can surpass it and can break law and have new technology. Let's meet at the next chapter.

CHAPTER FIVE

The Illutic Visionary

You have heard 'Illusion', right? This world is relative. It is not absolute. Everything is relative. This world is illutic as it seems. The things we see in this universe is so mysterious and our brain regenerates everything or imagine the things which are considered magical. Our brain is much powerful and can imagine something so mysterious that this creative mind awaits. Our imagining skills are capable of doing something very mysterious. The things that we see today, are these real? We see this world and the nature but, ARE THESE REAL? We can imagine everything if try to look closer and think deeply about that. Image forms in our mind that how the particular action can be performed before the actions even started! Are we imagining this particular world or something? Even we can imagine what is behind a particular phenomena and representing in the form of theory. Our ideas are infinite. One over another ideas will be formed after the previous ideas. This is so dreamy! Also, when we see dreams at night, why do we see it? Is there a connection to another world or something? It is now also a mystery. Dream is something where we can imagine something infinitely. There, we can keep every possible imagination. Dream is like something that connects to some other position of the negative universe, according to my view. Astrology says that there is meaning behind the dreams. But, they are not true, I think. Because, of course, I haven't experienced any of the predictions. But some people experienced the truths of these beliefs. Are there more living beings like us or some negative energy hits us? Dreams are the mysterious places where, you think something deeply, it appears in your imagination in the dream. So mysterious! It is very complex to solve as no one can view inside someone's dreams or no one can track from where or how the dream is being imagined. Illusion creates everywhere. Illusion meets imagination. Sometimes, a particular imagined thing comes in your own visualization. Sometimes, when someone imagines a thing, it creates a fake image in your visualization. It mostly happens when we go deep inside for some particular topic and reach beyond to visualize it. This explains - Illutic Visionary. But the main thing is, how do we imagine or visualize a dream? Does it give us a clue about connecting to some other worlds or something that is happening in the other worlds? Even if I repeat this question, it is not something easy to solve. Again remind you, I am not talking about astrology! Something bothers us to connect to other worlds in space-time. Our brain has something, or else how can we see those. But every dream that comes does have some meaning or else what is the use and meaning of the dream? Like we imagine a bucketful of stress in one spot when we sleep. Something is interconnected with this universe or interconnected to some particular worlds. This is also not usual. Sometimes, you don't dream or visualize something. It mostly happens on a sad day or on a moody day. Means when the day is something special. Just see the theory of Relativity. It also explains that every observer has different conclusions of an activity or phenomenon. For the receiver, it is different and for the observer, it is different. It is also a type of illusion. Mostly, these things are considered paranormal but Illusion is not paranormal. Its science. But how does this illusion create? If we do some medical studies, there is a part in our brain which displays dreams in our mind but what does it actually mean? It always displays new and extraordinary virtual reality. It has some extent which can surely be solved in the future. For now, we can ask some big questions for the upcoming crucial answers in the future. Unlike these, time is also an illusion. Because you can't see time even though it has only a single dimension. Because it is mixed with the 3 dimensional space. You know blackholes? They have a gravitational field so powerful even light can escape. The escape velocity of the light is not sufficient for escaping those massive blackholes. The blackholes are very dark only because of its gravitational field, like, these are also made up of stars and have the ability to emit light but its own gravitational field doesn't allow its light to emit. Time in the blackhole is nearly 0. If you go under it, it will have a 0 value or time. To escape these massive blackholes and warp time itself, illusion should be created as time is not possibly seen. Or time can take a route which will take us to the illutic world or to the past. To warp time, objects like wormholes can help with it. According to Einstein's general theory of relativity, Einstein's rosen bridge can help to go to the past. This also creates an illusion. The gravitational field is the weakest force if we compare it with the other three forces. But if we say some advantages related to gravitation, then it will be considered as the most advantaged force as it can cover a very long distance to hold up the bodies like our sun can hold up and orbit the other 9 planets (now pluto is not considered). Time is an illusion in this whole relative world. It is a relative world because not every scene is the same for different observers. We now also don't have any absolute unit for this world. We just consider seconds, minutes and hours. But what is the time of this universe? This is why we call this world a relative world because nothing is completely real. It's an illusion.

Conclusion

Let's talk about some mysterious events that happened in space. Like some mysterious sound waves, phenomena, etc. This research was mainly for the study of different dimensions and some branches involved with this theory. The last one (unit) ILLUTIC VISIONARY is more about some imaginary visions we relatively see. Even we create some extra illusions with our mind. We find our world as it is because of the light that shines the colours of this beautiful world. It is so nice to see this world, its nature, and its various phenomena. As we had come across the terms PARADOXES, MULTIVERSES AND DUALVERSES, DIMENSIONS and ILLUTIC VISIONARY, we have known about some 'beyond' imaginations, we also have discovered some more various things to 'imagine' about this world. We can't even finish discovering this world as it has everything that we wish to have. This universe has matter and antimatter, blackholes, whiteholes, and many craftings done by some materials. Some people are now also imagining some fictional sciences like aliens, spaceships, an object that can create anything and the creator of this universe! But if you think something deeply in your mind by observing it, it can be real or it can be there. It depends on your imagination skills and thoughts. Laws of physics can prevent it from saying that time travel is not possible because no object or even any particle can't exceed the speed of light. But then also time travel is possible as some scientists thought about the existence of blackholes which can have a gravitational force that can exceed the speed of light and the escape velocity of the light will decrease. Like these imaginary things like blackholes, science is made possible to go beyond the laws of physics or break it. So, to achieve any solutions, we have to imagine more and more so that we can achieve this science fiction as real and break the laws of physics. This path is not easy as everything you imagine will not become real as we are in a normal dimension where we also have some limited imaginations and thoughts. So, proper evidence is also needed to break the laws of physics. "Mind can do anything you want, just have a strength in it, whether it is a higher dimension or not, our thoughts are not limited."